PHOTOGRAPHING WILDFLOWERS

Techniques for the Advanced Amateur and Professional

CRAIG AND NADINE BLACKLOCK

VOYAGEUR PRESS

To Andy Gilats of the Split Rock Arts Program,
who first enlisted us into the role of photography instructors
—and whose encouragement and support over the years have been greatly appreciated.

Published by Voyageur Press
123 North Second Street
Stillwater, MN 55082

Distributed in Canada by Raincoast Books
8680 Cambie Street
Vancouver, B.C. V6P 6M9

ISBN 0-89658-069-5

Printed in South Korea
99 00 01 02 03 10 9 8 7 6

PRECEDING PAGE: *The foliage of many tropical flowers can be used as the primary design element.*

ABOVE: *We found these small white lady's slippers almost hidden in dead grasses that were glistening in full sunlight and blowing about in a stiff breeze. We carefully removed some of the grasses, then used the Diffusion Tent to block out the wind and soften the contrasty light. The background was shaded with a black cloth taped to the Diffusion Tent.*

Contents

Preface

OPPOSITE: *Whenever we can, we incorporate more into a photograph than just flowers. This gnarled log surrounding Indian paintbrush helps put the flowers into the context of their habitat near timberline in Colorado, as well as being visually interesting.*

Each winter we plan for our spring photography, resolving not to add too many flower photographs to our already bulging files.

And each spring our resolution melts away as surely as the last drifts of snow. We once again lie on our stomachs photographing the same patches of hepaticas that fill our backyard, trilliums that carpet nearby woodlots, jack-in-the-pulpits and marsh marigolds that line the streams, the group of yellow lady's slippers that appears between two fallen elms, and on and on. It seems that we are going to be photographing wildflowers forever.

Perhaps it is because flowers are evanescent. If we don't photograph them the moment they appear, it may be too late. So we chase one bloom after another until the woodland canopy closes out the sky and we focus our cameras on other subjects.

Having critiqued the work of student photographers for a number of years, we have found that closeup photography is the hardest area of photography for most people to master. This is natural, since many problems are magnified in closeup photography. Yet, by spending a little more time and implementing a few easy-to-use techniques, you will find wildflowers as rewarding to photograph as landscapes.

We prefer to work with available light and simple equipment. In this book you will find the things we have found most helpful to our students—things we use each spring in our own work. Their use is explained and diagrammed, so you should be able to easily apply these methods to your own photography.

Sometimes, though, circumstances require the use of extra equipment or advanced techniques to produce a fine photograph, so you will also find information on strobes, combining lenses, and more. In addition, the appendix gives technical information and formulas for further understanding and experimenting with closeup work.

We wish you many years of enjoyment and success photographing wildflowers and other treasures on the forest floor.

FIGURE 1-1

1 / Finding a Subject

FIGURE 1-1. *Where and when can you find round-lobed hepaticas? The inclusion of last year's red oak and bracken leaves in this photgraph helps the viewer answer these questions.*

It may sound silly to talk about finding a subject. Most wildflowers are brightly colored and easy to spot. But when it comes to finding flowers that make good photographs, the hunt can become a challenge.

If you live near a wild area, you will be able to keep an eye out for the different blooms. If you are not so fortunate and need to travel some distance, you must rely on someone else or on field guides to let you know when and where flowers you are interested in are blooming. Phone calls to park naturalists or botanical groups can save you the disappointment of arriving at the wrong time.

When you find flowers you want to work with, spend time walking and observing before actually setting up. We carry little markers that will help us find flowers we want to go back to.

What should you look for? This is a personal decision, but generally look for flowers in their prime and in a setting that makes a strong composition. This may be a simple group of two or three blossoms, or it may include other elements such as a fallen branch, a rock ledge, or a stream. We try to include things that will help the viewer learn where the flower grows and when it blooms. For instance, if we are working with some of the early blooming woodland flowers, we may include some of the previous year's tree leaves in the composition. This not only conveys the time (early spring) but under what species of trees the flowers are found (see figure 1–1).

Once you have found a subject, it is often necessary to do some "selective gardening." Some photographers refuse to do this. We have no problem with it as long as the intent is to strengthen the image you first found, not to create a composition that could never be found in nature.

Most of the time selective gardening involves nothing more than removing a few strands of dead grass from the background, where they can be distracting. When you look at a subject with two eyes it may look good, but if you close one eye, seeing the composition the

FIGURE 1-2A

FIGURE 1-2B

FIGURE 1-2A. *Sedges and dead sticks, although a natural part of this composition, detract from what we want to feature.*

FIGURE 1-2B. *Having selectively gardened out the distracting items, the subject matter is preceived more clearly.*

way the camera does, it may appear busy and confusing. Selective gardening removes the nonessential elements from the composition so the important lines come through clearly (see figure 1–2).

We do not condone the picking of wildflowers anywhere, and in many areas it is illegal. Some species, like the showy lady's slipper, require many years to reach blooming maturity. Work around such flowers with the utmost respect!

Working with any subject can easily flatten the surrounding vegetation and other flowers. Especially in public places, care should be taken to cause as little impact as possible. In some areas, even removing dead weeds may be against the rules. If at all in doubt, ask permission and about policies.

One of the most helpful things you can do is to record where and when you found flowers at their peak. If you are in an area that supplies trail maps, you can mark the species and dates right on the map, or you can make your own map and notes—anything that will allow you to find the same flowers in future years. At the same time, record what state of blooming other species are in. Because of differing weather conditions from one year to the next, the actual dates of blooming may change significantly, but the order that species appear will remain fairly constant. If you know a common flower blossoms at the same time as a rare one that you want to photograph, you can watch the common one's progress to know when to look for the rare one.

If you discover that you have arrived too late for a particular species, don't give up right away. It pays to look around. We have often found particular plants blooming many weeks after the majority of the species flowered. Check in low-lying, shaded cold spots where the season might have been delayed. But most importantly, make a note of when you think most of the flowers were at their best so you can get there at the right time the next year.

FIGURE 2-1

2 / Equipment

FIGURE 2-1. *By working with a composition of a number of flowers in a setting, it is possible to fill the frame with interest even if you only have a normal lens. Many of our pictures are taken from a distance that can be focused at with a standard 50mm lens.*

We frequently hear beginning photographers say how much they would like to photograph flowers but feel they can't because all they own is a normal 50mm lens. They may not be able to fill the frame with one violet blossom, but there are many splendid wildflower photographs that can be made with a simple camera, a normal lens, and a solid camera support. In fact, we photograph many of our flower pictures from a distance where we can use a normal lens (see figure 2–1). So even if you only own the most basic of equipment, you can start enjoying wildflower photography right away.

If you become serious about photographing wildflowers, you will eventually want to enhance your creative possibilities by acquiring some specialized equipment. Fortunately, most of this equipment also works for general photography, and we recommend keeping all your photographic needs in mind when selecting new equipment.

There is one item we place first on the list even if you only have a normal lens—a good tripod. The tripod is the foundation for sharp, vibration-free photographs. This is true for any photography, but is especially true for close-ups, where critical focusing and small apertures are required. We cannot stress strongly enough that consistently good closeup photography is not possible without a stable camera support.

Most wildflowers are small, and you will at times want to photograph them from near ground level. Many people use ground spikes or bean bags to support their cameras from this level, but we prefer a tripod that will hold the camera at any height and angle from ground level up.

To do this, a tripod must have a reversing center pole so the camera can be placed between the legs. The tripod head should adjust so the camera can be mounted right side up. Handles should not get in your way, and should function well. The tripod legs should be able to spread out, making room for access to the camera on one side and the subject on the other. We use the Bogen model 3021 tripod with the model 3028 head (see figure 2-2). This combination is versatile, and sturdy enough to hold a light 4 x 5 view camera.

You will need a cable release to trip the shutter without causing camera vibrations. An eight- or twelve-inch length works well, and we like to have a long one of about three feet for occasions when we need to stand away from the camera. We often wrap the long cable release around a tripod leg in a loose knot to keep it out of the picture and to further prevent vibrations from our hand being passed on to the camera.

While almost all of our landscape photographs are taken on 4 x 5 or 5 x 7 inch film, 35mm is ideal for flower photography, where extreme close-ups with large depth of field—the area which appears in focus—are often desired. The smaller film size uses much shorter lenses to achieve the same picture as a large format (for example, a 150mm lens on a 4 x 5 camera yields about the same image as a 50mm lens on a 35mm camera), and the shorter the lens, the more depth of field it has. We shoot some of the larger flowers or groups of flowers with a 4 x 5 camera, but as soon as the area of the composition gets smaller than about a square foot, almost all of the work is done with the 35mm camera.

Because the 35mm single lens reflex (SLR) camera with a through-the-lens (TTL) light meter is so perfect for flower photography, and is the camera most people use, we will confine the rest of the text to its use.

We could not begin to suggest which brand of camera to buy, as most recognized names are of very good quality. We can make some suggestions as to which options you might find most useful, and which might be a waste of money.

Most camera manufacturers make a complete line of lenses, but it is still a good idea to check out the total system (or those compatible) before deciding on a camera body.

Cameras with TTL meters offer one or more metering modes:

Manual: You set both the aperture and the shutter speed.

Aperture Priority: You set the aperture; the camera selects the shutter speed.

Shutter Priority: You set the shutter speed; the camera selects the aperture.

Program: The camera selects both the aperture and the shutter speed. (See figure 2-3.)

Because depth of field is vital to the look of a close-up and the aperture is one of the things affecting the amount of depth of field, it is important that *you* set the aperture. This means using manual or aperture-priority modes. A big advantage of the aperture-priority mode is that you don't have to keep adjusting the shutter speed if the light changes; the camera continually does it for you. You may want to have shutter priority included as a third option for other types of photography. The program mode is a total waste of money for anyone knowing anything about photography. Unfortunately, you may

FIGURE 2-2. *A versatile tripod is an absolute necessity. The Bogen model 3021 with the 3028 head has legs that can be spread extra wide, a two-section center pole, allowing the tripod to be set up low to the ground in the upright position, and a head that allows the camera to be mounted right side up when the center pole is reversed.*

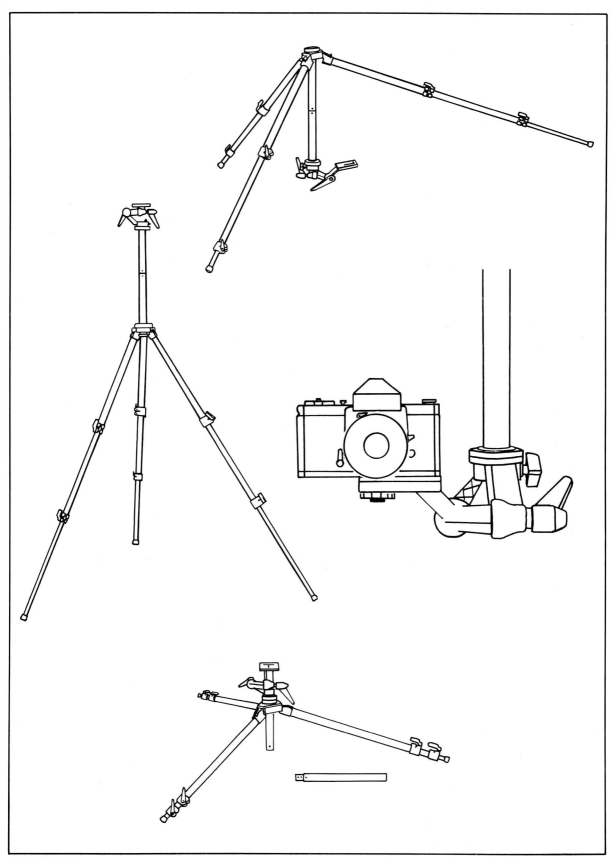

FIGURE 2-2

not be able to avoid having the program mode included with the other modes on the newer cameras.

With average close-ups, the meter reading will result in a correct exposure, but often you will need to give more or less exposure than the meter suggests. This is always possible with the manual mode, and on cameras that have an exposure compensation dial, it is easily done in the aperture-priority mode (see figure 2–4). Make sure you have some way to override the meter. If all else fails, you can always change the ASA setting.

TTL meters also vary in the area of the frame they read. The major types are listed below (see figure 2–5).

Averaging: All information in the frame is averaged equally.

Center Weighted: All information in the frame is averaged, with more emphasis given to the area in the center of the frame.

Spot: Only a very small spot is read. (With some cameras a number of spots can be read, and the camera will average them.)

Automatic Multi-Pattern: Light from different areas of the frame is read separately by the camera; this information is fed into a microcomputer that recommends the final exposure.

The spot meter gives the photographer the most information, control, and responsibility. The automatic multi-pattern meter delegates this to the camera, while the center-weighted system falls somewhere in between. All of these metering systems can be used accurately as long as the photographer understands what is being read by the meter and how and when to override what the meter recommends. No metering system is totally foolproof!

A motor drive is one option we have never felt necessary. You might find it helpful in critical closeup work where even the jarring of advancing the film by hand may move the camera out of position. But unless you also want it for other work, use the money for something else.

Auto-focus is as unnecessary as the program mode is in metering. First, your subject probably will not be centered, where the camera focuses, and secondly you are concerned about overall focus, from foreground to background, not just one spot.

There is probably nothing more confusing about purchasing equipment than trying to decide which of the dozens of lenses available are best for you. After quality, where you get what you pay for, the first think to think about is focal length. The focal length of modern lenses is given in millimeters. A 50mm lens is the normal focal length for the 35mm format. Focal lengths shorter than this take in a wider than normal angle of view, and those that are longer than 50mm take in a narrower than normal angle of view. The longer the focal length, the larger the subject matter will appear in the frame from any given distance.

The perspective you wish to work from is one determining factor in what focal length you need. Assuming you keep the subject the same size in the frame, you will use a short lens from a close distance

FIGURE 2-3. *Many new cameras offer four metering modes: (P) program, (S) shutter priority, (A) aperture priority, and (M) manual.*

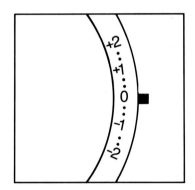

FIGURE 2-4. *An exposure compensation dial allows you to override the through-the-lens meter when it is working in one of the automatic metering modes. Setting the dial to the plus side will lighten the exposures, setting it to the minus side will darken them.*

In order to use your through-the-lens meter correctly, you must know what area of the frame it is metering.

FIGURE 2-5A. *AVERAGING METER—All of the light in the frame is averaged.*

FIGURE 2-5B. *CENTER-WEIGHTED METER—All the light in the frame is taken into the reading, but much more emphasis is given to the area in the center of the frame.*

FIGURE 2-5C. *SPOT METER—Only the light in the small spot is metered.*

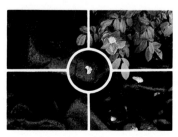

FIGURE 2-5D. *AUTOMATIC MULTI-PATTERN—Light from each section of the frame is read separately, then fed into a microcomputer.*

and a longer lens from a greater distance. This change in perspective will change the look of the picture.

With a close perspective and short focal length lens, the elements of the composition near the camera appear much larger than the background ones because there is a large difference in their relative distances from the camera. With a perspective from farther back and a longer focal length lens, the near and far elements of the composition appear much closer to the same size because their separation distance is relatively insignificant compared to the distance they are from the camera (see figure 2–6).

By moving closer or farther from a single subject, the subject can be made the same size with any lens, but the area of the background, if there is one, will be greater with a short focal length than with a long one. Thus, the amount of background you want to include may determine what focal length you will want to use (see figure 2–7).

Depth of field in close-ups (when infinity is not involved) does not change with the different focal lengths as long as the size of the subject in the frame is kept the same by adjusting the camera-to-subject distance.

There is one drawback to using longer than normal focal lengths: camera vibration is magnified. Extra precaution should be taken in mounting the camera solidly on the tripod and making sure to use the cable release. With a 300mm or longer lens, mount the lens rather than the camera on the tripod. Lock up the mirror if your camera has this option. In some cameras, the mirror flips up at the beginning of the self-timer cycle; however, tripping the shutter in this manner does not allow you to control the exact moment of the exposure, a problem if there are intermittent breezes affecting your subject.

We have taken wildflower photographs with extremely short and very long focal lengths, and nearly everything in between. Most of the time our needs can be met with three lenses: 28mm, 55mm, and 105mm.

Once you have determined the focal lengths you will want, you must find a way of focusing close enough with these lenses to get pleasing photographs of even small flowers. (With shorter than normal lenses, you can usually focus close enough without anything special added.)

The following items can help you focus close enough with normal or longer than normal lenses:

Extension Tubes: Any lens will focus closer with an extension tube placed between it and the camera (see figure 2–8). The tube is simply a rigid spacer with no glass. Tubes come in different lengths which can be added together if necessary—the longer the extension the closer you can focus. Longer focal lengths need more extension than short ones to achieve the same magnification. For example, to get a life size, 1:1 reproduction ratio, a 100mm lens would require a total bellows extension (the extension already existing in the lens and the camera plus the additional extension of the extension tube) of 200mm, while a 50mm lens would require only 100mm total bellows

FIGURE 2-6A

FIGURE 2-6B

FIGURE 2-6C

The perspective a photograph is taken from changes the way the foreground and background elements relate to each other.

FIGURE 2-6A. *This photograph was made with a 28mm lens from a very close perspective. As the diagram shows, the distance that separates the thistles from the black-eyed Susans in the background is greater than the camera-to-subject distance. Thus, the thistles appear much larger, and there is a perceived depth to the photograph.*

FIGURE 2-6B. *This photograph was made with a 55mm lens from approximately twice the distance as the one made with the 28mm lens. The content of the photograph has not changed much, but as the diagram shows, the camera-to-subject distance is now greater than the distance from the this-tles to the black-eyed Susans. Compared to the photograph made with the 28mm lens, the thistles and black-eyed Susans are now much closer to the same size, and the perceived depth is diminished.*

FIGURE 2-6C. *This photograph was made with a 105mm lens from approximately twice the distance as the one made with the 55mm lens. Now the distance that separates the thistles from the black-eyed Susans is insignificant compared to the camera-to-subject distance. Thus, both flowers appear equal in size, as if they were on the same plane. All sense of depth has been lost. Depth-of-field remained equal in all three photographs because as the focal lengths were doubled, so were the camera-to-subject distances (the magnification remained constant).*

extension. Most extension tubes automatically couple the diaphragm of the lens with the camera. Your camera manual will tell you how to meter using extension tubes. You may have to use "stopped-down metering" (see "Stopped-Down Metering" in the Appendix).

Extension Bellows: These function exactly the same as an extension tube only the bellows are flexible, allowing for adjustment of their length (see figure 2–9). Their bulk and fragility make them less practical in the field than extension tubes, and few automatically couple the camera and lens diaphragm.

NOTE: *Both extension tubes and bellows increase the distance of the lens from the film and thus reduce the intensity of the light hitting the film. (This also happens when focusing close with macro lenses.) A TTL meter will read this light loss, but if you are using a light meter that is not in your camera, or are using strobes, you must adjust the exposure to compensate (see "Bellows Extension" in the Appendix).*

Supplementary Closeup Lenses: These are single element lenses that screw into the filter mount of regular lenses (see figure 2–10). They come in different strengths measured in diopters. A +1 diopter lens mounted on any lens focused at infinity will change it so that it is focused at 1 meter, a +2 at ½ meter, and so on. You can then focus closer by extending the lens in the normal focusing manner. These lenses can be added together if needed, with the combined strength being the sum of the combination. For example, using the +2 and the +4 together would yield a +6, making the lens focus at ⅙ meter when set at infinity.

Supplementary closeup lenses have the advantage of not robbing you of light, since they do not add any bellows extension. They are not optically perfect, however, and should be used with smaller apertures if overall sharpness is desired. At wide-open apertures they can create beautiful, soft, halolike effects.

Macro and Micro Lenses: Lenses designed optically and mechanically to work well in the closeup realm without attachments are by far the best choice for closeup work (see figure 2–11). They are called macro, or sometimes micro, lenses and have the ability to focus from infinity down to about a 1:2 reproduction ratio (see figure 2–12), and extension tubes or bellows can be added for greater magnifications. Macro lenses have apertures as small as f/22 or, more commonly, f/32, allowing you adequate depth of field in tight close-ups.

While not all focal lengths are available in macro designs, you will have no trouble finding 55mm and 105mm focal lengths, which are good for general photography as well. Special macro lenses designed exclusively for closeup photography are available in focal lengths from 12.5mm to 38mm.

Zoom Lenses: Although great progress has been made in zoom lens quality, and many zoom lenses are labeled as macro lenses, these lenses generally do not focus as close as fixed focal length macros, nor do they always have the small apertures needed. In addition, they can be awkward and confusing to work with on close-ups.

There is also a common problem of gravity shifting the zoom if the lens is pointed down. We have taken good, sharp wildflower photographs using a zoom lens but whenever possible prefer to use a fixed focal length macro.

Combining Lenses: You can achieve very high magnifications by combining a primary lens (the one on your camera) of a medium long focal length with a reverse-mounted lens of a shorter focal length. The reversed lens is left wide open, and the aperture is controlled by the primary lens. The two can best be joined using a male to male threaded adapter (see figure 2–13). You can easily see what each combination can do for you simply by holding the reversed lens against the one on your camera. If you like a combination, tape them together and take some test shots, then if you are still happy, invest in the adapter. We do not personally use this method often since we are not interested in extreme close-ups.

Rack-and-Pinion Focusing Rail: When taking tight close-ups, it is essential that you be able to make slight adjustments in camera position. Moving the tripod can be very cumbersome. By mounting a focusing rail on your tripod and the camera on the focusing rail, small in and out adjustments can be made easily (see figure 2–14).

The following items can help you control lighting:

Diffusion Tent: This is by far the most useful lighting accessory—a canopy of translucent plastic specially treated to scatter the light passing through it, spread over a support of shock-corded poles (see figure 2–15). The tent softens the contrast of harsh sunlight and also acts as an effective wind break. It is also waterproof, allowing you to continue to work in a light rain.

Reflector: A reflector is used to bounce sunlight into shaded areas. We have found that the silver side of a space blanket makes an excellent, highly reflective, and lightweight reflector. If you're in a pinch, a white shirt or piece of paper can be used.

Black Cloth: A simple piece of black material about 4 x 5 feet can be used to cast shadows on backgrounds or can be placed on the opposite side of the subject from the camera to cut reflections off of shiny surfaces or water. The cloth is never placed in the picture area.

Other items to keep with your camera gear:

Duct Tape: A roll of duct tape will be of great help in the use of all of the above items. We find it essential in nearly all photographic work.

Kodak Grey Card: The grey card has an eighteen percent reflectance value. Reflected light meter readings taken off of it equal incident light readings. It can be used when there are no mid-tones from which to take a reflected light reading (see figure 4–1).

Nonphotographic items you might need include a backpack, rain suit, insect repellent, pocket knife (with scissors), wildflower guide, notebook, and pencil. If you are photographing in back country, be sure to include additional gear such as a compass, as well as food and water. Even if you only plan to shoot for a little while, it pays to take extra provisions along so that you have the option of working longer if the conditions warrant it.

You can control the amount of background taken into your composition by changing focal lengths.

FIGURE 2-7A. *This photograph was made with a short focal length lens from a close perspective. As the diagram shows, the short lens takes in a wide angle of view, which includes the sky and a large area of background.*

FIGURE 2-7B. *By doubling both the focal length and the camera-to-subject distance, the magnification is kept constant on the flower, but the amount of background included is cut down.*

FIGURE 2-7C. *By again doubling the focal length and the camera-to-subject distance, even more area of background is eliminated.*

FIGURE 2-7A

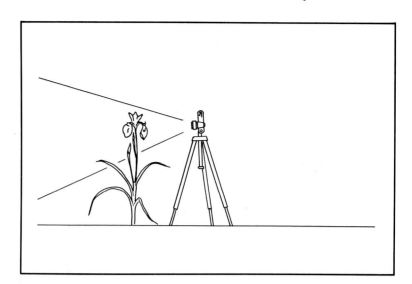

FIGURE 2-7B

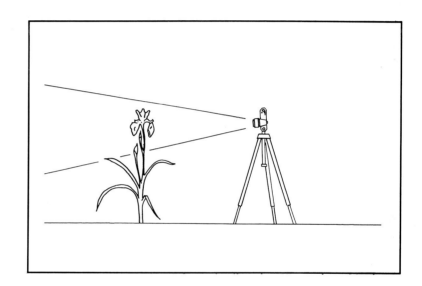

FIGURE 2-7C

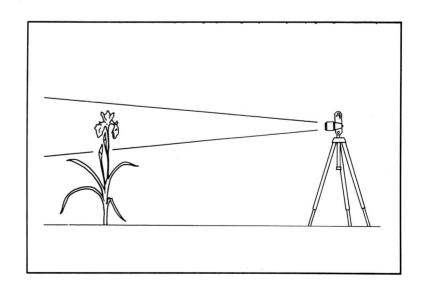

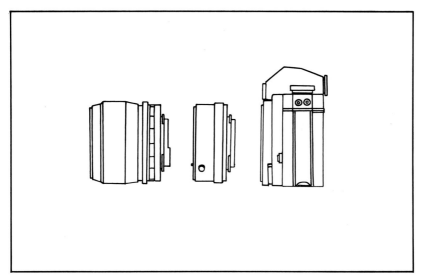

FIGURE 2-8

FIGURE 2-8. *An extension tube is a rigid spacer, available in different lengths, that is placed between the camera and the lens. It enables any lens to focus closer by putting the lens further away from the film.*

FIGURE 2-9. *A bellows is an adjustable-length spacer that functions similarly to an extension tube.*

FIGURE 2-10. *Supplementary closeup lenses screw onto the front of a lens like a filter.*

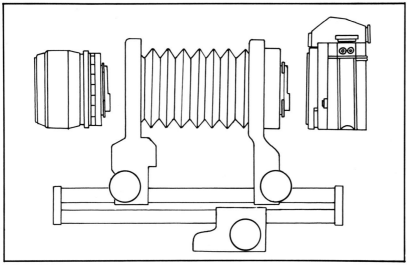

FIGURE 2-9

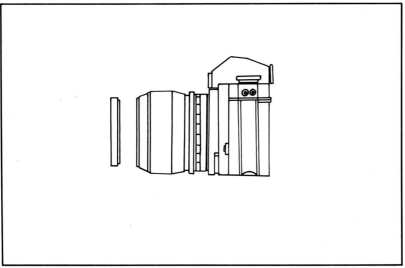

FIGURE 2-10

FIGURE 2-11. *Most macro lenses have enough built-in extension to reach a 1:2 reproduction ratio without added extension tubes or bellows. This, plus the fact they are optically designed for closeup as well as distant photography and have the ability to close down to f/32, makes them ideal for flower photography.*

FIGURE 2-12. *This wood poppy was taken with a 105mm macro lens at a 1:2 reproduction ratio.*

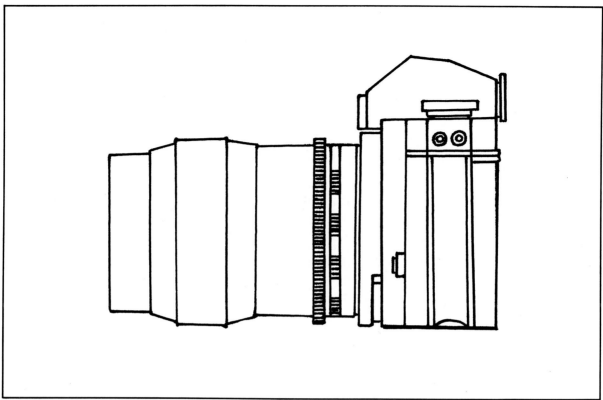

FIGURE 2-11

FIGURE 2-12

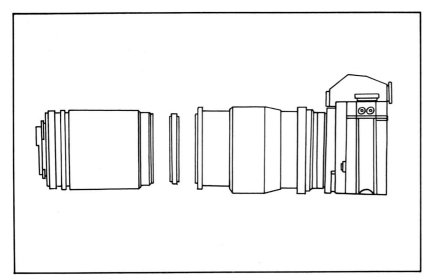

FIGURE 2-13

FIGURE 2-13. *A reverse mounted lens of a focal length shorter than the primary lens can be attached to the primary lens using a threaded adapter that screws into the filter mounts of both lenses. The combined lenses yield a highly magnified image. The shorter the reversed lens is in relation to the primary lens, the higher the magnification. The longer the primary lens is, the greater the camera-to-subject distance will be.*

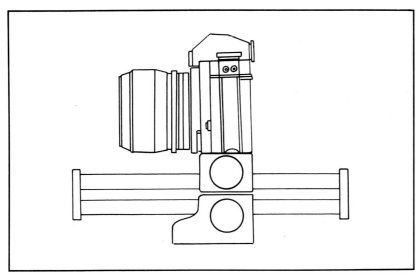

FIGURE 2-14

FIGURE 2-14. *With the camera mounted on a focusing rail and the rail mounted on a tripod, small camera-to-subject distance adjustments can be made without moving the tripod. This is a great advantage when working in high magnifications.*

FIGURE 2-15. *By using a Diffusion Tent, it is possible to work on sunny days and in a light wind. The diffusing plastic reduces the contrast by scattering the light and completely covers the working area to keep out breezes.*

FIGURE 2-15

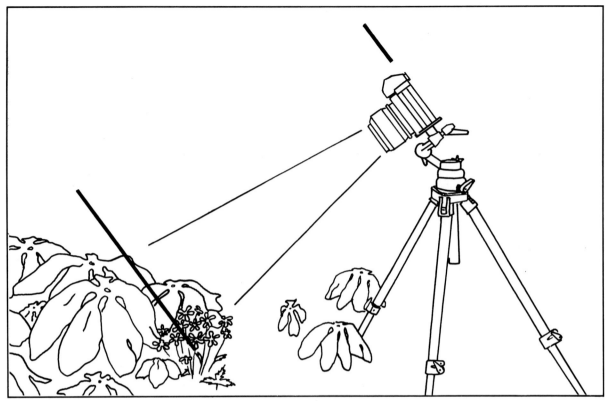

FIGURE 3-1A

FIGURE 3-1B

3 / Depth of Field and Focusing

FIGURE 3-1A. *In order to get the entire subject to fall within the depth-of-field, the camera has been positioned so the film plane and the plane of the subject matter are parallel.*

Because depth of field is extremely shallow in closeup work, it is important that you fully understand how to get the most out of it and how to focus critically.

In closeup photography, depth of field is determined by two things—the magnification (size of the subject in the frame) and the aperture.

The magnification is controlled by a combination of focal length and camera-to-subject distance. Depth of field changes inversely proportional to the square of the change in magnification. For example, a decrease in magnification by a doubling of camera-to-subject distance or a halving of focal length would each result in the subject appearing one half as large, with a net gain of four times more depth of field. In simple terms, the smaller the subject appears in the frame, the more depth of field you have.

Depth of field doubles every two stops the aperture is closed down (for example from f/11 to f/22). You have the most depth of field at the smallest aperture, which is usually f/22 or f/32. The aperture is the only control you have over depth of field that doesn't change the composition (other than changing film formats).

NOTE: *At a 1:1 reproduction ratio, the effective aperture is two stops smaller than marked. For example, f/32 is effectively f/64, since the diaphragm is twice as far away from the film as it normally is. This small an aperture will cause a slight loss of overall sharpness due to diffraction. Therefore, at 1:1 reproduction ratios or closer, you will not want to close down beyond f/22. At higher magnifications, you will need to use even larger apertures (see "Diffraction" in the Appendix).*

When you are first looking at a subject, it is important to think about what you want in focus. Try to compose your photograph so the areas you want sharp fall in one plane nearly parallel to the plane of the film (camera back). The thinner (less depth) this plane can be made, the less depth of field will be needed to get it all to appear sharp (see figure 3-1).

FIGURE 3-1B. *The overall sharpness of this image is the result of proper camera alignment, low magnification, proper focusing, and use of a small aperture.*

FIGURE 3-2A

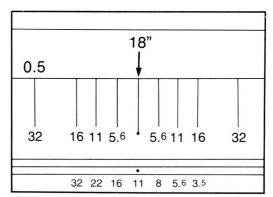

FIGURE 3-2B

With the following method, focusing and choosing the aperture become one operation. It shows you exactly what f-stop is needed for your depth of field so you don't close down further than necessary, causing the use of a slower shutter speed. We use this method for all of our 35mm work (see figure 3–2).

1. Focus on the nearest part of the composition you wish to be sharp. Note the distance you are focused at on the lens barrel by putting a fingernail on it and keeping it there.

2. Focus on the farthest part of the composition you wish to be sharp. Note that distance in the same way.

3. Turn the focusing ring until both the near and far distances fall within one pair of depth of field indication lines on the lens barrel.

4. Keep the lens focused at that point. Use the f-stop number indicated by the pair of lines outside of the two distances at which you focused.

NOTE: *Not all lenses have depth of field indication lines, especially not all zoom lenses. Look for them when buying lenses.*

If your near and far distances will not fit within the depth of field indication lines for even the smallest aperture on your lens, you cannot get enough depth of field to hold focus on everything you wanted to. You must then either recompose so that the plane of the subject is more parallel with the film plane or reduce the magnification. Remember that the depth of field is the area of acceptable sharpness. An element of the composition just outside of the depth of field may still appear quite sharp, and if it is in the background, may look fine, even though it is not as sharp as the subject.

Follow these steps to assure proper focus and aperture choice for desired depth-of-field:

FIGURE 3-2A. *Focus on the closest thing you want to appear sharp.*

FIGURE 3-2B. *Note that distance on the lens barrel.*

FIGURE 3-2C. *Focus on the farthest thing you want to appear sharp.*

FIGURE 3-2D. *Note that distance on the lens barrel.*

FIGURES 3-2E and F. *Rotate the focusing ring until both the close and far distances fall within one pair of depth-of-field indication lines. (As photograph E shows, not much will look sharp through the viewfinder.) Use the f-stop indicated by the lines that encompass the two distances.*

FIGURE 3-2G. The resulting photograph, focused precisely to get the most effective use of the available depth-of-field and taken at the exact aperture needed for the desired amount of depth-of-field.

FIGURE 3-2C

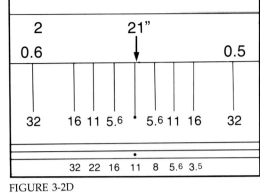

FIGURE 3-2D

FIGURE 3-2E

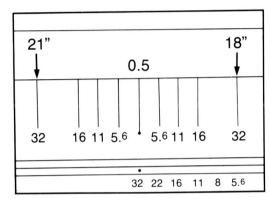

FIGURE 3-2F

FIGURE 3-2G

FIGURE 4-1A

FIGURE 4-1B

4 / Metering to Find the Shutter Speed

Once you have focused and found the aperture needed for your desired depth of field, you need to choose the correct shutter speed for the proper exposure.

You must understand how your meter works in order to get consistently accurate exposures. In chapter 2 we discussed different metering modes and the areas of the frame the different meters read. Now you must learn how to interpret this information.

The TTL meter is a reflected light meter. This means it reads the light values that are transmitted through or reflected off of your subject area towards the camera.

The meter is set to give an exposure reading that will render the area read as an eighteen percent reflectance grey value. This is a middle tone. Since most colored flowers and foliage look good rendered as a middle tone, the metering system works well most of the time (see figure 4–1).

But if the area of the frame the meter reads is filled mostly with a light subject such as a white flower, the meter will still treat this the same as anything it reads, rendering it as a middle tone, underexposing it and any darker background. In an instance like this, you must manually override the meter, giving more exposure than the meter suggests. How much more is a matter of some experience, but generally a one stop increase in exposure will be close to correct. If you are using the manual metering mode, slow your shutter speed by one stop; if you are using the aperture-priority mode, place the exposure compensation dial on +1 (see figure 4–2).

By the same token, if the meter is reading a frame filled with shadow or dark foliage and you have a small area of light flowers, the meter will render the dark area a middle tone and the flowers will be so overexposed that they will lack detail. Here you must manually override the meter by giving less exposure. Again, one stop will generally work, depending on how dark the background is in relation to the flowers. If you are in the manual mode, you set a one stop

FIGURE 4-1B. *If most of the area the meter reads is of an average middle value (eighteen percent reflectance grey), the system works fine. And since most closeup subject matter is close to this middle value, you can rely on the through-the-lens reading more often than not.*

faster shutter speed; if in the aperture-priority mode, you set the exposure compensation dial to –1 (see figure 4–3). If the background is very dark, you may want to meter off of a grey card instead of the composition. To do this, first focus on the composition as usual, choose your aperture, then place the grey card so that it fills the frame, being careful to hold it so it is in the same light as the subject and is not reflecting any glare into the camera. Then meter to find the shutter speed (see figure 4–4). If you do not have a grey card, you can meter off your hand. Average Caucasian skin is about one stop lighter than the grey card.

If you have a spot meter in your camera, you can read the flowers and the background areas independently and use the zone system to figure exposure. First focus, so that any light loss due to bellows extension will be incorporated into the meter reading. Next, meter the brightest thing in the composition. If this is a colored flower of a relatively middle value, you may only want to increase the exposure by about one-half stop from this reading. If it is a white flower, you may want to open up anywhere from one to two stops of exposure from this reading. After reading the highlight and choosing what you think will be the correct exposure for it, read a shaded area in which you want to record detail. Make sure this reading is no more than two stops underexposed from the exposure you have chosen. If it is more than two stops, it will appear nearly black. If you open up for the shadows, and the highlight reading is more than two stops overexposed from the exposure you use, the highlight area will lack detail. To learn more about using the zone system, read Ansel Adams's *The Negative.*

Remember, you have already picked the aperture for the correct depth of field and are now selecting the shutter speed for the correct exposure. Sometimes the correct shutter speed will be between marked speeds (for example, between ¼ second and ½ second). Some cameras work with the shutter set between speeds and some don't. If your camera set on manual will not work except on exact speeds, try the aperture-priority mode, which usually has a stepless shutter speed progression, using the exposure compensation dial if you need to override the meter. If you have no way of shooting between shutter speeds, then set the shutter speed to the slower speed and close down the aperture for the correct exposure. In this way you will not lose any depth of field.

If you want to bracket your exposure (taking one darker and one lighter shot in case you have made a mistake in figuring your exposure), we suggest that you do so by two-thirds of a stop rather than whole stops (see figure 4–5). To do this, after taking the photograph at what you think is the correct exposure, take one shot with the aperture closed down two-thirds of a stop from the original exposure. Then take one shot with the shutter slowed down one stop and the aperture closed down one-third stop from the *original* setting. In this way you have not opened up your aperture from that which you determined you needed for depth of field. If you have the

FIGURE 4-2A. *If the part of the frame your meter reads is filled with a bright area such as a white flower, the meter will treat this the same as anything it reads, giving an exposure reading that will result in an eighteen percent reflectance grey value. This photo is obviously underexposed, but the camera has no way to tell a white flower from a darker one. In this case, the meter must be overridden.*

FIGURE 4-2B. *By slowing the shutter speed to give one more stop exposure than the meter recommended, the white flower reproduces as a white flower and the surrounding values are improved as well.*

FIGURE 4-3A. *If the part of the frame your meter reads is filled with a dark area, the meter will again recommend an exposure reading that will result in an eighteen percent reflectance grey value. This will make the dark area look washed-out and completely burn out any highlight areas or white flowers. This time you need to override the meter in the other direction.*

FIGURE 4-3B. *By speeding the shutter speed up one stop from the meter reading, the proper exposure is achieved.*

FIGURE 4-2A

FIGURE 4-2B

FIGURE 4-3A

FIGURE 4-3B

FIGURE 4-4A

FIGURE 4-4B

FIGURE 4-4C

Sometimes there is not a large enough subject area from which to meter.

FIGURE 4-4A. In this example, the meter is reading the dark background, resulting in an overexposed flower. To solve the problem, you can take an incident meter reading or else introduce a middle-tone object from which to take a reflected light reading.

FIGURE 4-4B. *A grey card is placed in the frame in the same light as the flower. The meter reading is taken off of the grey card, resulting in the properly exposed flower in (C).*

camera in an aperture-priority mode, you can bracket using the exposure compensation dial, which will adjust the shutter speed without affecting your aperture at all. This is especially nice when using selective focus (see chapter 5).

If the light level is too low to get a meter reading with the aperture stopped down, set your shutter speed at the slowest speed it will read and open up your aperture to the correct exposure. Then close down the aperture to the desired f-stop for depth of field, counting how many stops this is. Slow your shutter speed by the same number of stops. The duration of the exposure doubles each stop. The progression of slow shutter speeds would go: ½ second, 1 second, 2 seconds, 4 seconds, and so on. When using these slow shutter speeds, you must be aware that the reciprocal arrangement between f-stops and shutter speeds no longer works. This problem is commonly referred to as reciprocity failure. You will need to give more exposure than the meter calls for (see "Reciprocity Failure" in the Appendix).

If these slow shutter speeds are not on your camera, set the shutter speed on B (bulb) and hold in the cable release during the entire exposure. Be careful to hold the release very still during the exposure, and watch the subject to make sure it hasn't moved during the exposure. Even a slight bobbing of a flower will result in a blurred image.

FIGURE 4-5. *Often you will want to bracket the exposure to cover a possible miscalculation or equipment failure. These photographs were bracketed by 2/3 stop intervals. 1/2 stop may not be enough, and 1 stop is often too much. By bracketing 2/3 of a stop, you are never more than 1/3 stop off.*

FIGURE 5-1A

FIGURE 5-1B

FIGURE 5-1C

FIGURE 5-1D

5 / Separating the Subject from the Background

Once the technical aspects of photographing close-ups are mastered, it is time to consider aesthetics—what do you want your pictures to look like?

Within the realm of wildflower photography, the possibilities for diverse compositional and technical styles are nearly limitless. Whatever styles you settle into, it is important that you ask yourself why you are making the photograph and what it is that you want to emphasize about your subject. Next, you need to learn methods that will let your feelings and unique ways of seeing come through cleanly to the viewer.

One of the problems that often muddles a photographer's statement is that the flowers become lost against the background.

Below are a number of ways to separate the subject from the background, each with a different effect. Some lend themselves to other areas of photography as well, where you have probably already used them.

Overall Focus: Often just having everything in the composition sharp will make it easy to read. It may help to think of this type of picture as a miniature landscape. Overall focus is usually used in pictures where a number of flowers or clumps of flowers are shown. The low magnification, a small aperture, and composing the picture so the film plane and plane of the composition are nearly parallel combine to accomplish the overall sharp focus (see figure 5–1A).

Selective Focus: Sometimes a flower is situated in such a way that you cannot have it large enough in the frame and still hold focus on the rest of the composition. Having the background just a little bit out of focus can be very distracting. This type of situation can be enhanced with selective focus. You isolate the subject flower from the background by using a very shallow depth of field so only the subject is in sharp focus (see figure 5–1B).

To do this, first compose the picture so only the subject is parallel to the film plane and focus on the subject. Look through the camera with the depth of field preview button held in and turn the aperture open and closed until the depth of field is sufficient to hold focus on the entire subject but shallow enough to throw the background far enough out of focus so it does not compete with the subject.

You may find you prefer longer than normal focal length lenses when using selective focus. The depth of field will not be affected (unless a distant background is included, which is sometimes the case with selective focus), but you will have less background area in the picture. If you are photographing from a low angle and want to eliminate the sky, for example, a longer lens might help (see figure 2–7).

You can and should use the light and dark or colored areas of the soft background as part of your composition. Keep the preview button pushed in while you are doing your final composing. Remember to keep the f-stop you found to be right for the selected depth of field and change only the shutter speed for exposure adjustments. (Using the aperture-priority metering mode may be helpful in this instance.) If you are unsure of what depth of field will look best, you can bracket the depth of field by changing the aperture. Remember to make the appropriate change in shutter speeds or your exposures will be off. For example, $\frac{1}{4}$ second at f/32, $\frac{1}{8}$ second at f/22, and $\frac{1}{15}$ second at f/16 would all be the same exposure but would result in progressively less depth of field.

Diffusion Filter: A diffusion filter is helpful on occasions when you want to use selective focus but closing down the aperture enough to hold focus on the subject brings the background too much into focus (see figure 5–1C). We started making our own "filters" a number of years ago; you can do the same. Take a piece of waxed paper and cut out a disc that covers the front of your lens. Start by making about a one-eighth inch hole in the center and then make cuts out from the hole about one-half inch until you have a hole the shape of a many-pointed star (see figure 5–2). Place the filter in front of the lens, being careful not to scratch the glass. The closer it is to the glass the better. Look through the camera with the depth of field preview button held in and the aperture set at the widest open setting that will still hold focus on the subject. Move the filter until the subject is clearly seen through the hole and then tape the filter to the metal part of the lens. You may need to make further cuts to custom tailor the filter to your lens and subject. Try different apertures to see what effect the change in depth of field has when using the filter. We found the filter works best on a normal focal length lens with an aperture around f/8. You might also wish to experiment with colored diffusion filters, especially green, to give the look of shooting through out-of-focus foliage.

Contrasting Background: One of the easiest ways to set off a subject, whether it is against a soft or a sharp background, is to compose the picture so the subject is against a contrasting color or value (see figure 5–1D). This is done by isolating flowers against the sky, or a red flower against green leaves, or most often by using a shaded background. You can create your own shade with your body, by hanging

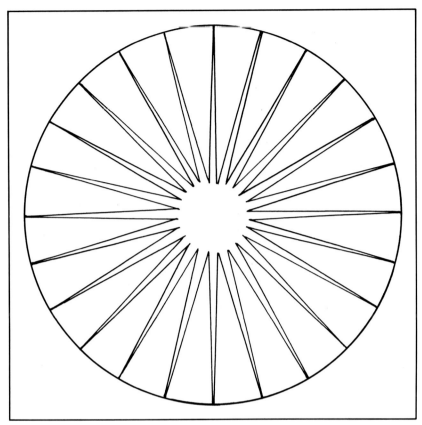

FIGURE 5-2. *A diffusion filter can easily be made from waxed paper. Start with a piece large enough to cover the front of your lens, then cut a many-pointed star shape from the center of it as illustrated. You can custom trim the opening to the individual composition. The filter is then taped in front of the lens.*

FIGURE 5-2

the black cloth on the Diffusion Tent, or by doubling up a portion of the Diffusion Tent to create a soft shadow. You are not trying to achieve a black background, just one that is a stop or two darker than the subject.

Think about the subject and how each of the above methods of separating it from the background would make it look. Generally, one will seem more appropriate than the others. You may in time come to favor one or two of these methods as having the look that fits into your overall photographic style.

Whichever of the separating methods you use, it will be more effective if you first try to compose the picture so that the different elements do not overlap each other. We often say that a good composition should fit together like a loose-fitting jigsaw puzzle, with a defining space between each piece.

FIGURE 6-1A

FIGURE 6-1B

6 / Lighting

FIGURE 6-1A. *Full sunshine usually results in contrasty, confusing close-ups.*

FIGURE 6-1B. *The results of softening the light with a Diffusion Tent and separating the subject from the background by shading the background with a black cloth taped to the Diffusion Tent.*

What light is best for wildflowers? Traditionally, the answer is overcast days for working with woodland flowers and sunny days for prairie and desert flowers.

The reason for preferring overcast lighting in the woods is that film cannot record both the deep shadows and the highlights found in the woods on sunny days. On cloudy days the light is more even, making exposures easier to figure and compositions less busy. The soft shadows that do exist on cloudy days can be recorded full of detail instead of as black holes, and highlights retain delicate textures and colors without burning out. There is, of course, the drawback of working in a lower light level, which means you will need to use longer exposures.

For many years, we photographed woodland flowers almost exclusively on cloudy days. Now we have come to prefer sunshine! The device that changed our thinking was the Diffusion Tent. The tent is made of a high-diffusion, translucent plastic that greatly softens the quality of the light. The highlight areas are reduced by about ½ stop and the shadow areas are raised about 2 stops. Most exposures remain the same with the Diffusion Tent as in full sun, but the photographs look as if they were taken on an overcast day, with soft, feathered shadows, and just a hint of highlights (see figure 6–1).

The Diffusion Tent becomes the framework for a miniature lighting studio. You can double up some areas to slightly shade a background, or tape the black cloth to it to create a darker background shadow, or tape a reflector to one side to add bounce fill.

Always get the camera into position first, then set up the supporting poles by sticking them in the ground. Drape the plastic over the top, staking it down to the ground to cut out the wind. Look through the camera carefully to make sure you are not getting the tent in the photograph.

If you are photographing a larger area, the Diffusion Tent can be hung between two trees like a sheet.

FIGURE 6-2. *Full sun was hitting this purple clematis from the left. A reflector was added to the right to bounce light back on the shaded side. A Diffusion Tent and black cloth were used to shade the background.*

When working with full sun on desert flowers or other subjects out in the open, a reflector comes in handy for filling shadow areas (see figure 6–2). Remember, the closer the reflector is to the subject, the more light it will bounce onto it. Make sure you get it close enough to do some good, but be careful not to overdo it. It is very easy to add too much bounce light and end up with a phony looking shot. Unlike the Diffusion Tent, which feathers out the edges of shadows, a reflector simply adds light to them. Edges remain sharp.

If you do not have a partner to help hold a reflector in place, you can use the Diffusion Tent poles or carry a second, light-weight tripod for this purpose.

FIGURE 6-3. *Sunlight transmitted through the petals of these poppies reveals much richer hues than reflected light would.*

Sometimes you will want to capture the rich transmitted light of sunlight through petals. In this case, adding bounce light to the picture will only detract from the quality you are after (see figure 6–3).

FIGURE 6-3

FIGURE 7-1

7 / Wildflowers in the Landscape

FIGURE 7-1. *By focusing at the hyperfocal distance for the smallest aperture of shorter-than-normal focal length lenses, it is possible to get very close to foreground flowers and still include infinity in the depth-of-field. This scene in Organ Pipe National Monument was taken with a 28mm lens at f/22.*

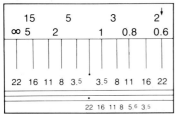

FIGURE 7-2A

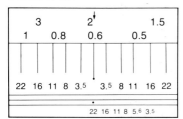

FIGURE 7-2B

To take a photograph like the one in figure 7-1, you must know how to set the focus at the hyperfocal distance for the smallest aperture.

FIGURE 7-2A. *This is easily done by placing the infinity mark over the depth-of-field indication line for the smallest aperture. The hyperfocal distance is the distance you are now focused at, and the near limit of the depth-of-field will be one half the hyperfocal distance. It will be found above the other depth-of-field indication line for your smallest aperture.*

FIGURE 7-2B. *Refocus at this near limit distance and move up to your foreground until it is in focus. This distance will be your near limit of depth-of-field. Refocus at the hyperfocal distance and take your picture at the smallest aperture. Everything from the foreground through infinity will be within the depth-of-field.*

So far we have been concerned with photographing small groups of flowers or even single blossoms. Sometimes fields of flowers absolutely demand the whole scene be photographed. Too often, the viewer of these photographs sees only the landscape, not the flowers, because the photographer has failed to feature the flowers as an important part of the composition.

You can feature the flowers by photographing a closeup foreground of wildflowers while at the same time taking in a sweeping landscape as a background. To do this, you need to use a shorter-than-normal focal length lens, such as a 28mm (see figure 7-1).

To find out how close you can focus with any lens and still have infinity in focus, turn the infinity mark on the focusing ring to the depth of field indication line for your smallest aperture. Look at the other depth of field indication line for the same aperture and see what distance it indicates. This is your maximum depth of field with that lens (you are focused at the hyperfocal distance for your smallest aperture). The shorter the lens, the closer you will be able to get to the foreground, making it bigger in relation to the background (see "Hyperfocal Distance" in the Appendix).

Once you have found the closest distance you can use (the near limit of the depth of field when focused at the hyperfocal distance), focus on that distance and move your camera in until the closest part of your composition comes into focus. Next, refocus so that the infinity mark is at the depth of field indication line for your smallest aperture and close down to that aperture (see figure 7-2). Figure your exposure to find the shutter speed and take your picture. (Since you have to use a precise f-stop, you may want to use the aperture-priority mode to control the shutter speed.) This type of photograph has a great sense of depth to it, and the near-far elements generate an immediate impact on the viewer. Obviously, you cannot control the lighting of an entire landscape, so it is important to think about the scene and choose the time and type of day carefully. In most cases, you will want to work in early morning before the wind comes up.

FIGURE 8-1

8 / Putting It All Together in the Field— A Summary

FIGURE 8-1. *Get into a routine of thinking about each step of making a photograph before you set up. This will help you avoid problems and become more creative. Once you have finished, record how you arrived at what you did. The more detailed your records, the faster you will gain an understanding of what is working and what is not.*

It seems that wildflower photography is a never-ending series of compromises. Getting an image with impact may mean moving in close to a flower. Doing this reduces the depth of field. Close down the aperture to increase the depth of field and the shutter speed slows down to where the wind is a problem or reciprocity failure makes for even longer exposures.

Unless we know from the start what lies ahead, it is easy to plow headlong into a situation that will force us to start all over again. Photographing with a fluid, sure sense of purpose and getting the results first envisioned can only come after mastering the technical concepts and much time spent practicing the craft.

When starting out, it is best to follow a checklist until the process is automatic. Below is such a list. Record everything you can about your first attempts—nothing will be a better teacher than your successes and mistakes, as long as you know how you created them. Record how decisions were made, don't just write down shutter speeds and f-stops.

1. Find your subject. Examine it from lots of angles. How would you like to define it? How will you separate it from the background? What technical problems will you encounter? Can any problems be solved by the way you compose the picture?

2. Find the perspective you want to shoot from and choose the lens that will fill the frame with the composition from that perspective. Look through the camera until you have the exact spot you want to shoot from and then set up your tripod and mount the camera.

3. Fine tune the composition, including any selective gardening of the subject area that might be needed (if allowed).

4. Control the lighting (if needed and possible) with the Diffusion Tent, black cloth, or a reflector.

5. Focus and choose your aperture for depth of field.

6. Figure your exposure to find the shutter speed. Do you need to override the meter? Is reciprocity failure involved?

7. Watch the flowers with both eyes (not through the camera) for subject motion. When everything is still, trip the shutter with the cable release.

8. If in doubt, bracket the exposure. Reexamine what you have done and *record it.*

FIGURE 9-1A

9 / The Forest Floor—What's Out There Besides Flowers?

FIGURE 9-1A. *Here the sunlight has been softened with two layers of the Diffusion Tent. The composition includes a number of mushrooms as well as a pine needle and a leaf, thus filling the frame without needing a high magnification. The film plane and the plane of the subject matter are nearly parallel, reducing the amount of depth-of-field required for overall focus.*

FIGURE 9-1B. *One common mistake people make is taking mushroom pictures in direct sunlight. As with flowers, harsh sunlight and shadows detract from an image.*

It would be a shame if we limited our hands-and-knees photo excursions to flowers. The techniques you have just learned for working with wildflowers work just as well for all sorts of closeup subjects. Let's look at a few of the common and not so common nonflower subjects that might catch your eye, and what special considerations you will have to give them.

Fungi: Just as the woodland flowers are fading away, the mushrooms, puffballs, and other members of the fungi world begin to make their appearances. The variety of colors and shapes rivals even the flowers. We are reminded of the popularity of fungi as subject matter each time we teach by the number of students who bring mushroom pictures to be critiqued. Unfortunately, only a handful are any good. What is it that makes mushrooms so hard to photograph?

Most of the photographs fail in one or more of three areas: sufficient depth of field, composition, or appropriate lighting. The tendency of most photographers is to zero in on a fungus. As a result, they end up using a high magnification with the accompanying lack of depth of field. Since most fungi are quite deep, there is no plane with which to line up. No matter what angle the picture is taken from, if the frame is filled with the fungus, focus cannot be held from the front of it to the back. (Selective focus on a subject such as a mushroom seldom looks good.) The only way to solve the depth of field problem is to reduce the magnification. By backing up, you can perhaps photograph a group of fungi, or use other elements as you have learned to do with flowers, to fill the frame (see figure 9–1).

The contrast problems are no different here than with flowers. They can be solved with the Diffusion Tent or a reflector. Sometimes you will find that the leaves which now cover the woodland canopy cut out too much light for an available light exposure. If your exposure times start running into 20 seconds or longer, you may wish to use a strobe (see chapter 10).

Berries: Blueberries, cranberries, crowberries, baneberries, bunchberries, rose twisted-stalk, jack-in-the-pulpit; a shiny, colorful array of late-summer fruits waiting to be photographed. Those that grow low on the ground are easy to work with, others that hang on the end of long stems bobbing in midair are a difficult challenge even to professionals.

Unless the background is a long way from the subject and can be kept way out of focus and the berries kept sharp, use overall focus. A clump of berries that gradually gets soft, or a half-soft background looks bad.

If it is sunny, soften the light with the Diffusion Tent. If you separate the subject from the background by shading the background, add a reflector to the far side of the berries, bouncing light toward the camera. This will add a highlight to the edges, defining them against the dark background.

As with mushrooms, don't succumb to the tendency to center one clump. Instead, stay back and work with a number of berries or foliage around them. This will help with depth of field and make for more interesting compositions (see figure 9–2).

When photographing berries that hang on trees or shrubs, try to arrange the foliage around them to fill the frame on the plane of focus. In this way, you will not have background areas falling out of focus.

You may need to tie a supporting brace to a long stem or branch to keep it from waving about in the wind.

Mosses and Lichens: The patterns, strange shapes, and brilliant colors of mosses and lichens look like they were designed by Dr. Seuss. Few subjects are as interesting to explore with a macro lens, and few photographs as fun to show, simply because so few people have every really gotten down on the ground to discover what they've been walking on.

The easiest way to photograph mosses and lichens is to work from a distance that shows the patterns of their growth. Most of the time, you will find that everything is nearly on one plane, so focusing is very easy (see figure 9–3). You would be missing a great deal, however, if you did not also move in tight to show the intricacies of these subjects. As you do, you will discover that what appeared as one plane from three feet away is really a mountainous terrain from three inches away. Focusing now is extremely critical, and depth of field very limited. As with fungi and berries, selective focus does not work well with mosses and lichens, so finding a composition with the elements nearly in one plane only a fraction of an inch deep is important. Lighting should be soft, to show the subjects off without confusing shadows (see figure 9–4). The exception to this would be lichen patterns on rock faces, where full sun helps bring out the textures.

Ferns: Ferns are perhaps the most difficult of closeup subjects to photograph. The two things that draw us to ferns are hard to show in the same shot—their graceful shapes and the detailed outlines and

FIGURE 9-2. *The first response of many photographers is to fill the frame with one cluster of berries. The results often look like they came from a fruit company catalog. In the case of this photograph of bluberries, a very low magnification was used, making it easy to hold everything within the depth-of-field. The inclusion of the dead logs makes this a distinctive, visually exciting photograph rather than just another bunch of berries. It was taken in direct sun under a Diffusion Tent.*

FIGURE 9-2

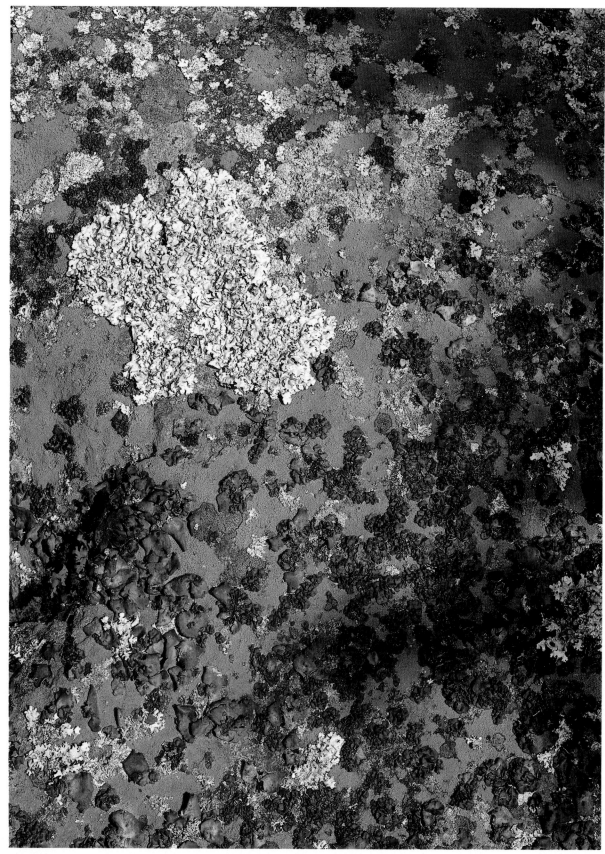

FIGURE 9-3

FIGURE 9-3. *Growth patterns of lichens on rocks are easily photographed. Everything is nearly flat, making focusing easy. A strong cross-light helps bring out the textures of the rock and lichens.*

FIGURE 9-4. *Extra effort is required to hold everything sharp when in this tight on tiny mosses and lichens, but it can be done.*

FIGURE 9-5. *Ferns are often easier to photograph if you include groups of them or other surrounding vegetation to reduce the magnification needed. A cloudy day will provide beautiful, even light.*

FIGURE 9-4

FIGURE 9-5

textures of the individual fronds. Their deep shapes make for a depth of field problem, and any wind starts them waving.

Ferns must almost always be photographed on a cloudy day. The light is soft, and there is less chance of wind. Most fern pictures fall within three categories: the whole fern or group of ferns, a wide angle shot showing the detail of frond ends while also showing the rest of the plant (usually looking down into the fern), and a detail of one frond.

As with any closeup subjects, the farther back you can stay, the easier it will be to get everything in focus. So, if you want to show the whole plant, try to show a number of plants together (see figure 9-5).

If you wish to try the wide-angle approach, don't look right down into the center of the fern, but work from one side, with the closest frond at the near limit of your depth of field and the ground at the far limit. Put the center of the fern in either the upper right or left, not in the center of the frame.

Close-ups detailing part of a frond work best with selective focus. Make sure your camera back is parallel to the frond, close down the aperture enough to hold focus on the fern, but keep the background a soft blur.

Moving Water: Whenever you include moving water in your composition, you must think about what shutter speed to use. The shutter speed determines how much the water will be blurred. Shutter speeds of ⅟₃₀ and ⅟₁₅ second make the water look the way we normally perceive it. Water photographed at shutter speeds slower than ⅟₁₅ second looks progressively more blurred until becoming foglike at speeds slower than a second; shutter speeds faster than ⅟₃₀ second make the water look progressively more frozen, until at ⅟₅₀₀ and ⅟₁₀₀₀ seconds every droplet is nearly stopped in midair.

If there is sun on the water, the scintillations will produce lines the length they traveled during the exposure; these lines will be long streaks at slow shutter speeds and small sparkles at fast shutter speeds. There is no one correct way to photograph moving water. The two photographs in figure 9-6 are different, yet neither one is better than the other. Learn how light and shutter speeds affect an image with moving water in it, then choose the variables that will produce the look you want.

Leaves: From the opening of buds in the spring through frost-rimmed leaves on the ground in the fall, plant and tree leaves provide photographers with wonderful shapes and forms.

As with flowers, almost any technique works well with leaves, but usually one will be better in any given situation. Think about why you like a particular leaf: is it the shape, the lighting, the color? Then think through all the possible ways you could treat it and which one would best bring across your intentions (see figure 9-7).

Ice: The world of close-ups doesn't have to end in the fall. Winter macro photography can be just as rewarding as summer macro pho-

FIGURE 9-6A. *Photographed in shade, there are no highlights on this water. A 3 second exposure resulted in the water appearing blurred.*

FIGURE 9-6B. *Sunlight hitting the water produced scintillations that reproduced as streaks the length they traveled during the ⅟₁₅ second exposure. Although this photograph is closer to the way we would perceive the water, it is a matter of personal choice as to which is the more pleasing interpretation.*

FIGURE 9-6A

FIGURE 9-6B

FIGURE 9-7A

FIGURE 9-7B

Three views of an autumn woods:

FIGURE 9-7A. *We are used to viewing the world from eye level, thus photographs taken from this perspective have a comfortable, familiar feeling to them.*

FIGURE 9-7B. *By getting down and working in detail, a photographer can reveal textures and patterns most people overlook.*

FIGURE 9-7C. *An even more unusual perspective of the forest floor produces an image few of us have seen since we rolled in the leaves as youngsters.*

FIGURE 9-7C

FIGURE 9-8

FIGURE 9-9. *Feathers are flat enough to permit extreme close-ups and still hold focus on the whole subject. This photograph of a mallard feather was made with a 105mm lens reverse-mounted on a 135mm lens (see figure 2-13) and lit from the side with a strobe.*

tography. It takes a little more looking to find subjects in the winter, but they are out there.

We especially enjoy working at the beginning and end of winter, when puddles and small ponds are freezing and thawing, with a new pattern to the fresh ice each morning (see figure 9–8). Frost crystals, icicles, and snowflakes are all potential subjects.

Ice and snow are subjects where high contrast usually helps, not hurts, the photograph. If you work just after sunrise and before sunset, the shadows will be longer, and the sunlight warm, contrasting with cool blue shadows. Sharp focus is the rule, defining the crisp subjects.

Remember that with the overall brightness of snow and ice, you will need to override your TTL meter and give more exposure than it calls for. For most scenes, slowing the shutter speed one stop will give an appropriate exposure.

Feathers: Whether a stray found on the forest floor or one obtained through hunting, feathers offer the photographer many possibilities. Taken in a setting, they can be treated much the same as flowers; removed from context, extreme close-ups reveal abstract textures and patterns that sparkle like jewels. Because feathers are fairly flat, it is possible to use high magnification and still retain overall focus as long as the plane of the feather and the film plane are exactly parallel. A strong crosslight from either the sun or a strobe will help bring out the texture (see figure 9–9).

FIGURE 9-8. *Ice is one of the few subjects where high contrast light helps. This photograph was made just as the first rays of the morning sun came skipping over the surface.*

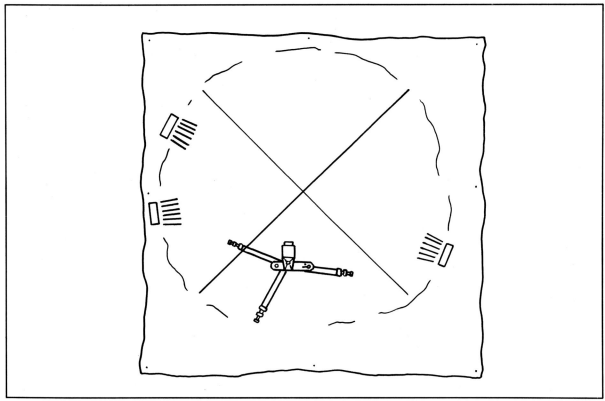

FIGURE 10-1

FIGURE 10-2

10 / Using a Strobe with the Diffusion Tent

FIGURE 10-1. *A typical setup using a strobe with the Diffusion Tent. The camera is set on bulb and the shutter held open with a locking cable release. A single strobe is then popped off manually from a number of positions from outside of the Diffusion Tent; then the shutter is closed. The available light must be low enough that it does not affect the exposure during the time the shutter is open.*

We seldom use a strobe, and when we do we don't want the results to look like we did.

In order to get strobe illumination to look like overcast available light, two things are necessary. The light must be soft to avoid the exaggerated contrast and deep shadows associated with strobe exposures, and the illumination should be even from the front to back to avoid the telltale falloff of light that many strobe-lit pictures have.

The first problem is easy to solve. The Diffusion Tent, set up in the normal way, scatters a strobe light just as it does sunlight. By manually popping the strobe off from a foot or so outside the tent, the light will be soft and the shadows well lit.

The second problem, that of even illumination, requires a little more effort. If your subject area is small and the strobe is a few feet away, you probably will not have a problem. If, on the other hand, you have a large area to illuminate, you will need more than one strobe or need to use more than one pop of the same strobe from more than one position.

If you are only using one strobe, simply put the shutter speed on bulb and keep the shutter open with a locking cable release. Pop the strobe off however many times you wish, and then close the shutter. The available light level should be quite low to allow you to keep the shutter open long enough (see figures 10–1, 10–2).

Each time you double the number of pops of the strobe, you have increased the exposure by one stop. For example, if one pop of the strobe gave enough light for f/16, two would be correct for f/22 and four for f/32. Remember to add in any bellows extension when figuring the exposures and to allow recycling time between pops of the strobe. A strobe meter that adds up the accumulated strobe light is very helpful.

As with sunlight, the Diffusion Tent does not have a significant effect on the net exposure. Highlights will be reduced a little and shadow values raised a lot. As with any strobe work, experiment and record your first efforts until you work out a formula for your equipment and working methods.

FIGURE 10-2. *In order to make this photograph look like it was made in overcast light, a strobe was popped off three times from different positions outside a Diffusion Tent, as in figure 10-1.*

Appendix

BELLOWS EXTENSION

NOTE: *If you are using a TTL meter, you do not need to compensate for bellows extension. The meter in the camera already has.*

There are a number of ways to figure the amount of light loss due to the extension of the lens away from the film; below are three of them.

Method 1: Focus on your composition and adjust the TTL meter for a proper exposure and note what it is. Then leaving the camera in position, refocus on infinity, and adjust the meter for a proper exposure. The amount you had to close down from the first reading is the amount of light you are losing to bellows extension. For example, if your first reading when focused on the composition was ⅕₅ second at f/5.6 and your second reading when focused at infinity was ⅕₅ second at f/8, the bellows extension is costing you one stop of light.

Method 2: To use a math equation, you must first know how to measure the bellows extension. A simple method is described below.

1. Measure the distance from the camera back to the front of the lens barrel when the lens is focused at infinity.
2. Measure the same distance when the lens is focused on your subject, including any extension tubes or bellows.
3. Subtract the first measurement from the second and add the focal length of the lens. This is your total bellows extension. Use the formula below to find the extension factor. (You can also use the above method to find the total extension possible with your various lenses, to find out how much extension will need to be added in the way of extension tubes to achieve desired magnifications.)

$$\frac{(bellows\ extension)^2}{(focal\ length)^2} = extension\ factor$$

Multiply the exposure time from your meter reading by the extension factor to get the shutter speed for the correct exposure.

Method 3: If you know the magnification you are using, you can convert it to the extension factor using the following formula, or refer to the chart below. The reproduction ratio is often printed on the lens barrels of macro lenses, it appears as: 1: 10 9 8 and so on. In the formula, S = the second number in the reproduction ratio.

$$\frac{(1+S)^2}{S^2} = extension\ factor$$

Example: *1:8 reproduction ratio* $\dfrac{(1+8)^2}{8^2} = \dfrac{81}{64} = 1.26$

REPRODUCTION RATIO	BELLOWS EXTENSION FACTOR
1:8	1.26
1:6	1.36
1:4	1.56
1:2	2.25
1:1	4
1:.5	9

Multiply the exposure time from your meter reading by the extension factor to get the shutter speed for the correct exposure.

DIFFRACTION

A gain in magnification moves the aperture blades physically farther away from the film, effectively changing the f-stop:

$$f\text{-stop} = \frac{focal\ length\ of\ lens}{diameter\ of\ aperture}$$

The use of any *effective* f-stop much larger than f/45 or f/64 will cause an overall loss of sharpness due to diffraction. Below is a table of the smallest useful apertures when used with these reproduction ratios:

REPRODUCTION RATIO	SMALLEST USEFUL APERTURE
1:1	f/22
2:1	f/16
3:1	f/11
5:1	f/8

FACTORS

Filters and bellows extension formulas often give the amount you must correct for light loss as a "factor." To use these factors, you multiply the original exposure time by the factor to come up with the corrected exposure time. For instance, if your original exposure time was ¼ second and your bellows extension factor was 4, you would use a corrected exposure of 4/4, or 1 second. This is equal to two stops exposure difference. Often it is helpful to convert the factor number to stops. For quick reference, refer to the chart below.

FACTOR	EQUIVALENT STOPS
1.5	½
2	1
3	1½
4	2
6	2½
8	3
12	3½
16	4

HYPERFOCAL DISTANCE

This is the distance you focus at to get the maximum depth of field for any given f-stop. Infinity is always at the far depth of field limit and one half the hyperfocal distance at the near limit. You can figure hyperfocal distances for any lens and f-stop using the formula below. It uses a circle of confusion of .00125 inch (1/800 inch). If you are planning to enlarge your slides greatly, you may wish to substitute .001 (1/1000) inch. The formula starts with the focal length in millimeters and gives a hyperfocal distance in inches.

$$\frac{(mm\ of\ focal\ length^2 \div 625)}{(f\text{-stop} \times .00125)} = hyperfocal\ distance\ in\ inches$$

Below are some common lenses and the hyperfocal distances for their smallest apertures, figured at 1/800 inch circle of confusion:

FOCAL LENGTH	F-STOP	HYPERFOCAL DISTANCE	NEAR LIMIT OF DEPTH OF FIELD
18mm	22	19 inches	9½ inches
20mm	22	23 inches	11½ inches
28mm	22	46 inches	23 inches
50mm	16	16 feet, 8 inches	8 feet, 4 inches
55mm	32	10 feet	5 feet
105	32	36 feet	18 feet

RECIPROCITY FAILURE

As shutter speed times lengthen beyond about ½ second, the one-to-one reciprocal arrangement between f-stops and shutter speeds no longer holds true. Film manufacturers provide tables of time adjustments and filtration adjustments they recommend for long exposures. Below is a table we use for Kodachrome 64. We do not use correcting filtration, since we prefer to correct the color in printing, rather than add a filter when taking the original.

METER SAYS	ADJUSTMENT
1 second	open aperture ⅓ stop
2 seconds	use 3 seconds
4 seconds	use 6 seconds
8 seconds	use 16 seconds

STOPPED-DOWN METERING

Stopped-down metering means metering while the aperture is manually closed down to the aperture you are going to take the picture at. You do this by holding in the depth of field preview button or lever. If you are in an aperture-priority mode, you will need to hold the button in during the exposure (an awkward thing to do that can easily cause camera vibration). If you are in the manual mode, you only need to hold the preview button in during the meter reading—you can let it up before taking the picture. Check your camera and accessory manuals to see when and how to use stopped-down metering with your particular equipment.

Index

To make a Diffusion Tent:

The frame: Two or three ten-foot-long shock-corded fiberglass tent poles in five sections. Put ferrules on ends and crimp the tip to make a sharp foot that will protect pole and be easy to stick into ground.

The tarp: Ten foot by ten foot tarp. Either polyethylene or thin, white nylon. If you use polyethylene (sold as vapor barriers in lumber yards) you will need to abrade it with a nylon dish scrubber to make it scatter light. This will transmit more light that nylon, but will build up heat in the sun. Put grommets in corners and along edges half way between corners (use grommets with rubber washers made for plastic tarps).

Use four or more tent stakes to hold the tarp down in the wind. To secure the tent when rolled up and to string it between trees, get two small bungee cords (about eight inches long). All items except the tarp material can be found at camping supply stores.

ADDITIONAL BLACKLOCK TITLES ALSO AVAILABLE FROM VOYAGEUR PRESS:

Black Hills/Badlands: The Web of the West
Text by Mike Link; Photos by Craig Blacklock
8½ x 11, 120 pages, 96 color photos

Journeys to Door County
Text by Mike Link; Photos by Craig and Nadine Blacklock
8½ x 11, 136 pages, 105 color photos

Our Minnesota, Revised Third Edition
Text by Fran Blacklock; Photos by Les, Craig, and Nadine Blacklock
10 x 9, 128 pages, 92 color photos

OTHER GREAT PHOTOGRAPHY BOOKS FROM VOYAGEUR PRESS:

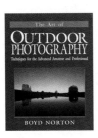

The Art of Outdoor Photography
By Boyd Norton
"Mr. Norton's new book is brimming with ideas, clever techniques, insights and encouragement for shooting in the outdoors." *The New York Times*
8½ x 11, 152 pages